ideals® MOTHER'S DAY

And so because you love me,
And because I love you, Mother,
I have woven a wreath of rhymes
Wherewith to crown your honored name:
In you not fourscore years
Can dim the flame of love,
Whose blessed glow transcends the laws
Of time and change and mortal life and death.

Christina G. Rossetti

ISBN 0-8249-1034-6 350

Publisher, Patricia A. Pingry
Editor/Ideals, Kathleen S. Pohl
Managing Editor, Marybeth Owens
Photographic Editor, Gerald Koser
Staff Artist, Patrick McRae
Research Editor, Linda Robinson
Phototypesetter, Kim Kaczanowski

IDEALS — Vol. 42, No. 3 March MCMLXXXV IDEALS (ISSN 0019-137X) is published eight times a year,
February, March, May, June, August, September, November, December
by IDEALS PUBLISHING CORPORATION, 11315 Watertown Plank Road, Milwaukee, Wis. 53226
Second class postage paid at Milwaukee, Wisconsin and additional mailing offices.
Copyright © MCMLXXXV by IDEALS PUBLISHING CORPORATION.
POSTMASTER: Send address changes to Ideals, Post Office Box 2100, Milwaukee, Wis. 53201
All rights reserved. Title IDEALS registered U.S. Patent Office.
Published simultaneously in Canada.

SINGLE ISSUE — $3.50
ONE YEAR SUBSCRIPTION — eight consecutive issues as published — $15.95
TWO YEAR SUBSCRIPTION — sixteen consecutive issues as published — $27.95
Outside U.S.A., add $4.00 per subscription year for postage and handling

*Front and
back covers
LILACS
Gene Ahrens*

Needs

I want a little house
   Upon a little hill,
With lilacs laughing at the door
   When afternoons are still.

I want an apple tree
   Laden with drifts of bloom;
I want blue china all about
   In every little room.

I want a little path
   Bordered with brilliant phlox,
And on each windowsill I want
   A painted flower box.

And then — I want you there
   In sun, and frost, and rain,
To smile when I come trudging home
   Through a dim, scented lane.

For what's a little house
   Upon a little hill,
Unless you light the fire for me
   When nights are strangely still?

Charles Hanson Towne

Photo opposite
WILLIAMSBURG, VIRGINIA
H. Armstrong Roberts

Mother's Garden

Mother is envied by the neighbors
For the flowers she has grown;
They all say her garden
Is the loveliest they've known.
In early spring she will prepare
A fertile, sunny spot.
How carefully she marks the rows
And plants the seeds she bought.

Her garden seems to thrive and grow
Beneath her tender care,
For it is watered with her love
And nourished with a prayer.
God answers her with sun and rain
And as the months go by,
The flowers bloom in radiant hues
Like rainbows in the sky.

Her prize bouquets are freely given
To those who chance to call...
But to the ill and lonely folks
She gives the best of all.
For brightening other people's lives
Is Mother's lifelong goal...
And the beauty of her flowers
Is reflected in her soul.

Reginald Holmes

Mom's Day

Mom, it is your day once again
So I've picked a rose from the few
That bloom outside my windowpane
To send especially to you —

To tell you just how very much
I love you on this special day,
How memories of your soft touch
Cheer me, although you're far away.

Ocie Tackett Lay

Tribute to Mothers

Anna Reeves Jarvis lived most of her life in the small town of Grafton, West Virginia. She raised eight children with the same strength and spirit that later propelled her into action and service in her community.

At twenty-six, Mrs. Jarvis set out to improve the unhealthy conditions she saw in Grafton and neighboring towns. She visited the local churches and called upon every woman to join her in improving such unsanitary living conditions in the area. Working with doctors and nurses, Mrs. Jarvis's Mother's Day Work Clubs, as she called them, were successful in their duties of inspecting all milk for children, helping mothers with tuberculosis, and furnishing medicine to the poor.

Because of their commendable work record, the Mother's Day Work Clubs were called on again during the Civil War. Generals Lee and McClellan both sent their wounded to Grafton. Mrs. Jarvis responded with aid and the promise that both armies would be treated without discrimination. Her organization received high praise for its magnificent efforts.

In 1868, after the war, Mrs. Jarvis served her country with a Mother's Friendship Day Meeting. The object was to rebuild peace and harmony among the returning soldiers and their families. She instructed her club members to invite every soldier, Blue and Gray, to attend this meeting. On the appointed day, leading citizens approached Mrs. Jarvis and asked her to dismiss the group for fear of violence. She replied, "I will not. I am not a coward."

At the appropriate time, in front of a large crowd, Mrs. Jarvis and a friend appeared dressed in blue and gray. Proudly, Mrs. Jarvis explained the purpose of the Mother's Friendship Day. Then she called for the singing of some patriotic songs. By the time the songs were over, a feeling of unity had brought the participants together.

Throughout her years of service, Mrs. Jarvis wanted to establish a national Mother's Day. But she did not live to accomplish that goal. Her daughter Anna was working in Philadelphia when she received the news that her mother had died; Anna immediately began to plan for a Mother's Day.

She became involved in pursuing her mother's dream and devoted all her time to writing and speaking on the topic of a national observance. As a result of these efforts, the first official Mother's Day service was held on May 10, 1908, at a Methodist Church in Grafton. Five hundred white carnations were sent by Anna because they were her mother's favorite flower.

In 1914, Anna took her cause to Washington where she contacted various lawmakers as well as President Woodrow Wilson. Due largely to Anna's determination, on May 8, 1914, President Wilson approved the second Sunday in May as Mother's Day. He signed a resolution that stated, "The service rendered the United States by American mothers is the greatest source of the country's strength and inspiration." The President ordered that on Mother's Day the flag be displayed on all government buildings in the United States and its foreign holdings.

Anna did not take the credit for establishing a national holiday. "Without my mother's work, never would there have been a Mother's Day," she said. Mother's Day, now celebrated in forty-six countries around the world, "is in honor of the best mother who ever lived — the mother of your heart," Anna said.

Melanie Vickers

My Song

This song of mine will wind its music around you, my child, like the fond arms of love.

This song of mine will touch your forehead like a kiss of blessing.

When you are alone it will sit by your side and whisper in your ear; when you are in the crowd it will fence you about with aloofness.

My song will be like a pair of wings to your dreams; it will transport your heart to the verge of the unknown.

It will be like a faithful star overhead when dark night is over your road.

My song will sit in the pupils of your eyes, and will carry your sight into the heart of things.

And when my voice is silent in death, my song will speak in your living heart.

Rabindranath Tagore

Painting opposite
LORD OF THE MANOR
Edmund Blair Leighton
(Photo, Three Lions)

Reprinted with permission of Macmillan Publishing Company from COLLECTED POEMS AND PLAYS by Rabindranath Tagore. Copyright 1913 by Macmillan Publishing Co., Inc., renewed 1941 by Rabindranath Tagore. Also with permission of Macmillan, London and Basingstoke.

Mother - Prayer

"Lord, make my loving a guard for them
    Day and night;
Let never pathway be hard for them;
    Keep all bright!
Let not harsh touch of a thorn for them
    Wound their ease;
All of the pain I have borne for them
    Spare to these!"

So I would pray for them,
Kneeling to God
Night and day for them.

"Lord, let the pain life must bring to them
    Make them strong;
Keep their hearts white though grief cling to them
    All life long.
Let all the joys Thou dost keep from them
    At Thy will
Give to them power to reap from them
    Courage still!"

So I must ask for them,
Leaving to God
His own task for them.

Margaret Widdemer

What Mother Is

A song of hope, a fervent prayer,
A noble dream, and tender care;
A light of truth that makes me free —
All this my mother is to me.

A bank to put my worries in,
A balm to soothe my woes and sin,
A comforter where'er I be —
All this my mother is to me.

An eager heart my joys to share;
A valiant soul to bid me dare
The shining heights her eyes can see —
All this my mother is to me.

The one who loves with all her heart;
The one who always does her part
To help and guide so patiently —
All this my mother is to me.

An artist, poet, saint, and seer;
A fragrant flower, a memory dear —
My thoughts and words fail utterly
To tell what Mother is to me.

J. Harold Gwynne

Her Heart's at Home

She keeps her heart within four walls.
She does not send it out to roam
Where dust, like a dark shadow, falls
Upon a highway far from home.
She keeps her heart where, satisfied,
The tranquil joys of home abide.

She keeps her thoughts at home, content
With all the sweetness they distill.
They do not gather worriment
Upon a changing, distant hill;
She keeps her thoughts where they can be
Held in a white serenity.

She keeps her heart at home, secure
Behind familiar locks that bar
The hurting world. She is so sure
It is at home the real joys are.
She keeps her heart at home to bless
The ones she loves with happiness!

Anne Campbell

Queen Rose

The jessamine shows like a star;
    The lilies sway like sceptres slim;
Fair clematis from near and far
    Sets forth its wayward tangled whim;
    Curved meadowsweet blooms rich and dim —
But yet a rose is fairer far.

The jessamine is odorous; so
    Maid-lilies are, and clematis;
And where tall meadowsweet flowers grow
    A rare and subtle perfume is;
    What can there be more choice than these?
A rose when it doth bud and blow.

Let others choose sweet jessamine,
    Or weave their lily-crown aright,
And let who love it pluck and twine
    Loose clematis, or draw delight
    From meadowsweets' cluster downy white —
The rose, the perfect rose, be mine.

Christina G. Rossetti

Morning Wish

The sun is just rising on the morning of another day. What can I wish that this day may bring me? Nothing that shall make the world or others poorer, nothing at the expense of other men; but just those few things which in their coming do not stop with me but touch me rather, as they pass and gather strength.

A few friends, who understand me, and yet remain my friends.

A work to do which has real value, without which the world would feel the poorer.

A return for such work small enough not to tax anyone who pays.

A mind unafraid to travel, even though the trail be not blazed.

An understanding heart.

A sight of the eternal hills, and the unresting sea, and of something beautiful which the hand of man has made.

A sense of humor, and the power to laugh. A little leisure with nothing to do.

A few moments of quiet, silent meditation. The sense of the presence of God.

And the patience to wait for the coming of these things, with the wisdom to know them when they come, and the wit not to change this morning wish of mine.

Walter Reid Hunt

Flowers for Mother's Day

Bluebells blowing in the shade
Of an old mock orange bush,
Masses of purple lilac,
And clusters of field daisies,

The yellow roses and iris,
All the peonies full-petalled —
Give or take a flower or two
Depending on the season's sun and rain —

This is the flowering time,
The time of the fragile petal
And the sweet and subtle fragrance
Of the month of May.

Elizabeth Searle Lamb

Photo opposite
BLEEDING HEART
Jeff Wiles
Peregrine Photo Studio

Perhaps with Eve

I think it must have started long ago —
Perhaps with Eve — the urge of womankind
To feed the many hungers that we know
Of heart and soul, of body and of mind.

A bowl of pottage or a cup of tea,
A picnic luncheon for young love to share,
Some gay confection for a jubilee,
Or simple nourishment of homey fare,
Are more than what they seem, and more than food:

They are the substance of her love made real,
The impulse of a strong and generous mood
To cheer and comfort, to delight and heal,
And add, with woman's own special grace,
Clear honey to the bread of commonplace.

R. H. Grenville

Martha of Bethany

It's all very well
Sitting in the shade of the courtyard
Talking about your souls.
Someone's got to see to the cooking,
Standing at the oven all the morning
With you two taking your ease.
It's all very well
Saying he'd be content
With bread and honey.
Perhaps he would — but I wouldn't,
Coming to our house like this,
Not giving him of our best.
Yes, it's all very well
Him trying to excuse you,
Saying your recipe's best,
Saying I worry too much,
That I'm always anxious.
Someone's got to worry —
And double if the others don't care.
For it's all very well
Talking of faith and belief,
But what would you do
If everyone sat in the cool
Not getting their meals?
And he can't go wandering and preaching
On an empty stomach —
He'd die in the first fortnight.
Then where would you be
With all your discussions and questions
And no one to answer them?
It's all very well.

Clive Sansom

From THE WITNESSES AND OTHER POEMS by Clive Sansom, published by Methuen and Company, Ltd. Reprinted by permission of David Higham Associates, London.

Before the seed there comes the thought of bloom,
The seedbed is the restless mind itself.
Not sun, not soil alone can bring to border
This rush of beauty and this sense of order.

Photo above
MORNING GLORY
Jeff Wiles
Peregrine Photo Studio

"To My American Gardener, with Love" from the book POEMS & SKETCHES OF E. B. WHITE. Copyright ©
1981 by E. B. White. Reprinted with permission of E. B. White and Harper & Row, Publishers, Inc.

Flowers respond to something in the gardener's face —
Some secret in the heart, some special grace.
Yours were the rains that made the roses grow,
And that is why I love your garden so.

E. B. White

The Magic of Childhood

Know you what it is to be a child? It is to be something very different from the man of today.

It is to have a spirit yet streaming from the waters of baptism, it is to believe in love, to believe in loveliness, to believe in belief. It is to be so little that the elves can reach to whisper in your ear. It is to turn pumpkins into coaches, and mice into horses, lowness into loftiness and nothing into everything — for each child has his fairy godmother in his own soul. It is to live in a nutshell and count yourself king of the infinite space; it is

> To see a world in a grain of sand,
> Heaven in a wild flower,
> To hold infinity in the palm
> of your hand,
> And eternity in an hour.

Francis Thompson

Iris

Dainty fairies
   in my garden,
Working
   with infinite care,
Uncurled
   the lovely petals
Of satin
   and velvet rare.
With scattered
   dew and magic wands,
They changed
   the dark green stems
Into
   a royal family,
Wearing
   colored diadems.

Ona Jane Meens

Photo opposite
IRIS
Fred Sieb

Sleep, Baby, Sleep

Sleep, baby, sleep!
Thy father watches the sheep;
Thy mother is shaking the dream-land tree,
And down falls a little dream on thee:
Sleep, baby, sleep!

Sleep, baby, sleep!
The large stars are the sheep,
The little stars are the lambs, I guess,
The fair moon is the shepherdess:
Sleep, baby, sleep!

Author Unknown

Cottager's Lullaby

The days are cold, the nights are long;
The north wind sings a doleful song;
Then hush again upon my breast,
All merry things are now at rest,
    Save thee, my pretty love!

The kitten sleeps upon the hearth,
The crickets long have ceased their mirth;
There's nothing stirring in the house
Save one wee, hungry, nibbling mouse;
    Then why so busy thou?

Nay, start not at that sparkling light;
'Tis but the moon that shines so bright
On the windowpane bedropped with rain;
Then, little darling! sleep again,
    And wake when it is day.

Dorothy Wordsworth

Wynken, Blynken, and Nod

Eugene Field

Wynken, Blynken, and Nod one night
Sailed off in a wooden shoe...
Sailed on a river of crystal light,
Into a sea of dew.

"Where are you going, and what do you wish?"
The old moon asked the three.
"We have come to fish for the herring fish
That live in this beautiful sea.
Nets of silver and gold have we!"
Said Wynken, Blynken, and Nod.

The old moon laughed and sang a song,
As they rocked in the wooden shoe,
And the wind that sped them all night long
Ruffled the waves of dew.
The little stars were the herring fish
That lived in the beautiful sea.
"Now cast your nets wherever you wish . . .
Never afeared are we!"
So cried the stars to the fishermen three,
Wynken, Blynken, and Nod.

All night long their nets they threw
To the stars in the twinkling foam . . .
Then down from the skies came the wooden shoe,
Bringing the fishermen home.
'Twas all so pretty a sail, it seemed
As if it could not be,
And some folks thought 'twas a dream they'd dreamed
Of sailing that beautiful sea.
But I shall name you the fishermen three,
Wynken, Blynken, and Nod.

Wynken and Blynken are two little eyes,
And Nod is a little head,
And the wooden shoe that sailed the skies
Is a wee one's trundle bed.
So shut your eyes while Mother sings
Of wonderful sights that be,
And you shall see the beautiful things
As you rock in the misty sea
Where the old shoe rocked the fishermen three,
Wynken, Blynken, and Nod.

Life's a Puzzle!

Mothers can do many things,
As little boys all know:
They can untie knots in string,
Or make an Indian bow;

And they can patch a cut you've got,
Or pick a splinter out;
They can crack the hardest nut,
Or fry a rainbow trout.

A mother even seems to know
If you didn't wash your neck,
Or if you sneaked outside to go
Where she forbid, by heck!

And mothers bake the things you like
To eat the best of all!
They seem to know you broke your bike,
Or lost your brother's ball.

The only thing I want to know
Is how a mom so wise,
Can act so dumb by kissing me
In front of all the guys.

Saxon White Uberuaga

Favorite Things

The things that make a mother smile
    are things that make all life worthwhile:
A home that's filled with warmth and love
    and treasures that she's fondest of;
Little feet that make her day
    a busy world of work and play;

Friends who take the time to call,
    a door that opens wide to all;
A room that holds the morning sun,
    and laughter when the day is done.
The special joy that each day brings
    is made of Mother's favorite things.

Author Unknown

Readers' Reflections

A Mother's Love

There's a very special treasure
When there's love within a heart;
A mother's love is special
For it plays a vital part.

Time will never change it;
It will strengthen through the years;
Roots are deep because of love
Shared through joys and tears.

Cherished are our memories,
And now's the time to say,
"You are loved most deeply,
You're remembered everyday."

Patricia Vess
Garden City, Michigan

A Mother's Musings

I watch the snowflakes as they fly,
Myriads of them drifting by.
Each hexagon is crystal fine,
Filigreed in its own design.
But patterned snowflakes do not stay;
Warmed by sunshine they melt away.

All of my children come and go;
In my home they live and grow.
Although each child may be unique,
I know it's love all children seek.
Though they may grow up and away,
I'll put love in their hearts to stay.

Maurine Wagner
Peru, Indiana

Show Piece

Mary had a sweet old Gram
Whose hair was tinted blue;
And anything that Mary asked,
Gram was glad to do.

She followed Mary to school one day,
And at the opening bell,
Was introduced to Mary's class
As Mary's show and tell.

Phyllis Feuerstein
Olympia Fields, Illinois

Editor's Note: Readers are invited to submit poetry, short anecdotes, and humorous reflections on life for possible publication in future *Ideals* issues. Please send xeroxed copies only; manuscripts will not be returned. Writers will receive $10 for each published submission. Send material to "Readers' Reflections," P.O. Box 1101, Milwaukee, Wisconsin 53201.

Mother and Son

Forget the crumbs upon the floor
And gently close the kitchen door.
Hold his hand within your hand
And walk across the greening land.

Point to robin's bright red breast;
Watch the bluebird build her nest.
Stand where apple blossoms fall;
Hear the cardinal's friendly call.

This day was made for talk and fun
Between a mother and her son.

Elva Adams Schaub
Yellow Springs, Ohio

God's Angels

Mothers are the angels sent by God to touch our lives with the light and the warmth of His caring. Through their guidance, we seek and find the path to our future. By their inspiration we make our own contribution to life and posterity.

Edith Schaffer Lederberg
Lauderhill, Florida

Thanks Again, Mom

For music and laughter
And birthday cakes,
For the energy, patience,
And time that it takes

To love someone small
And help her to grow,
While teaching her all
That she needs to know,

For stories and kittens
And teddy bears,
For kisses and confidence,
Praises and prayers,

For all that you've done
And all that you do —
I just want to say,
"Dear Mom, thank you!"

Gloria Isbell
Bement, Illinois

Mother's Day Breakfast

Danish Lemon Twists

2 packages dry yeast
2 teaspoons granulated sugar
2 room temperature eggs, well beaten
¼ cup granulated sugar
½ cup warm milk (105°)
1 teaspoon vanilla
3¾ cups flour
2 teaspoons salt
1 pound unsalted butter, well chilled,
    cut in 1-inch pieces
1 egg, lightly beaten
1 tablespoon milk

To make pastry dough: Place yeast and 2 teaspoons sugar in bowl. Place 2 eggs in a measuring cup. Add warm water to eggs to measure ¾ cup. Pour over yeast mixture. Let rest 5 minutes. Add sugar, milk, vanilla, and ¾ cup flour. Stir until smooth. Cover with towel; let rise in warm area 2 hours. Place remaining 3 cups flour and salt in large bowl. Cut in cold butter with pastry blender until crumbs are the size of small peas. Lightly stir in yeast mixture just to incorporate liquid. (Butter must remain in pieces.) Turn onto floured board. Shape into 12-inch by 18-inch rectangle. Using spatula, fold one third of dough over. Fold another third over the first, forming three layers of dough, to yield a 4-inch by 18-inch rectangle. Cover with plastic; refrigerate for 10 minutes. Repeat rolling and folding process 3 times. If butter softens, refrigerate immediately. After final folding, refrigerate dough at least 1 hour, or up to 24 hours. Roll and shape into lemon twists.

To shape lemon twists: Cut dough in half. Roll one half into 8-inch by 21-inch rectangle on lightly floured board. Cut into ¾-inch by 21-inch strips. Use one strip to form each lemon twist. Twist strip about 10 times. Shape into a "U" with bottom end of "U" nearest you. With left hand, hold down top ends of "U"; with right hand holding curved bottom, twist dough twice, forming a large loop (twist should occur toward lower end of dough). With left hand, bring loose ends toward you so "twist" is in center, forming two loops. Ends should extend two inches below bottom of loops. Then pull ends under and through each loop, over the top; secure underneath, pinching dough, forming a figure eight. Place on greased baking sheet. Brush with mixture of 1 egg beaten with 1 tablespoon milk. Let rest 30 minutes. Brush again with egg mixture. Make depressions on each side of figure eight. Fill each depression with 1 teaspoon Lemon Curd Filling. Place in 450° F. oven. Immediately reduce to 400° F. Bake until golden brown, 12-15 minutes. While still warm, drizzle with Lemon Glaze. Yield: 10 twists.

Lemon Curd Filling

2 eggs
½ cup lemon juice
¼ cup water
¾ cup granulated sugar
1 teaspoon cornstarch dissolved in 1 teaspoon water
2 tablespoons butter

Beat eggs in small bowl. Combine lemon juice, water, sugar, and cornstarch mixture in heavy saucepan. Heat until sugar dissolves and syrup mixture begins to simmer. Drizzle ¼ cup of syrup into beaten eggs, stirring constantly. Pour egg mixture into saucepan. Cook over medium heat, stirring constantly until mixture thickens. *Do not boil.* Stir in butter until melted. Cool.

Lemon Glaze

1 cup sifted confectioners' sugar
1 tablespoon heavy cream
    Enough lemon juice to form a thin consistency

Mix together in bowl to smooth consistency.

Brie and Watercress Omelet

1½ tablespoons butter
1 small tomato, diced
2 tablespoons chopped watercress
    Salt, as desired
    Pepper, as desired
3 room temperature eggs
3 ounces Brie cheese, cut in thin slices

Melt ½ tablespoon butter in small sauté pan. Add tomato and watercress and sauté about 2 minutes. Season with salt and pepper. Set aside. Beat eggs in a small bowl. Melt 1 tablespoon butter in 6-inch nonstick sauté pan over medium high heat. Add eggs; immediately begin stirring eggs in small circular motions with a wooden spoon. Work very quickly so eggs do not have a chance to set on the bottom of the pan. When eggs are almost completely cooked, gently spread to edges of pan and cook 15 seconds to set bottom. *Do not brown.* Immediately remove pan from heat. Place tomato mixture and 2 ounces of sliced brie on one half of the omelet. Fold omelet over and slide onto plate. Garnish with remaining watercress, tomato, and cheese, if desired. Yield: 1 serving.

What Price?

Grandmother slaved for hours to prove
Her culinary arts.
She mixed by hand the pastry
For her jam and butter tarts.
With sweat of brow and elbow grease
She kneaded spongy dough,
But Mom just grabs a ready mix
To make a pretty show.

Gram swept the floor the corn broom way,
Then waxed and polished bright
Until each spot of lint and dust
Had vanished from her sight.
But Mom has almost dustless rooms,

Her vacuum whisks them clean;
Her polish shines while wiping on,
Leaves plastic-coated sheen.

Grandmother had a garden huge
And canned for days with care
Her home-grown fruits and vegetables
For family winter fare.
But Mom just runs across the street
To nearest market place,
There buys food frozen or in cans,
By package or by case.

(Time passes on, but this remains —
Our appetites ne'er seem to change!)

Irene Dyck

The Quilt

The pattern she chose was her mother's,
Each strip cut precisely by hand.
The colors she picked as she laid out the squares
Were those from a faraway land.

There was blue like the ocean she'd crossed
When she'd come to this place as a bride.
There was white from her aprons, and rose like her shawl,
And grey like the tears that she'd cried.

There was dark brown for sorrow (the year of the flood),
When the tilled earth had all swept away,
But next to this piece came a strip of green sprig —
Her bonnet from her wedding day.

There were red checks for kitchens, and yellows for joy,
All stitched and placed carefully to see.
Most people would view only colors and style,
But for her it was memory.

Meredith J. Cone

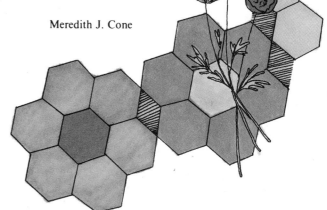

Fred Toothaker

Fred Toothaker was born on February 26, 1894, in Newark, Ohio. He was raised on a farm and later studied architecture, spending his professional life as an architectural engineer. The meticulous attention to detail required of Mr. Toothaker in his professional life served him as well in his chosen hobby — the crafting of rhyme and meter in his verse. Poetry was his relaxation, and he has said, "I get pleasure from seeing my work in print and from the thought that some folks may enjoy reading it."

Mr. Toothaker began writing in his early 40s, and his work appeared often in the local paper. Pen and pad were never far from him; he composed easily and whenever inspired. Frequently, his inspiration came from happy times spent with family and friends.

Not only has Mr. Toothaker contributed to *Ideals* but *Ideals* has played a small part in his personal life. The publication of a poem in these pages enabled some distant cousins from Texas to renew old acquaintances with the poet.

An Old-Fashioned Mother

I remember an old-fashioned mother;
  I remember the gray in her hair —
Just an old-fashioned mother with patience,
  And a brow slightly furrowed with care.
I remember the hoop skirts and ruffles,
  And remember the high button shoes.
Yes, I see her in checkerboard apron,
  Such as old-fashioned mothers would choose.

I recall all the meals so delightful
  She prepared for our table with care;
And on Sundays a feast more than special —
  Works of love for her family to share.

I remember the old-fashioned organ,
  And the hymns she so proudly would play
After dishes were done and the ironing
  Had been finished and all put away.

We were proud of that old-fashioned mother,
  And were grateful for kindness bestowed —
For the care and the deepest devotion
  From a heart that with love overflowed.
May we always have old-fashioned mothers,
  And be ever so proud of them, too;
For it's mothers like one I remember,
  That will help our ambitions come true.

My Mom's a Baseball Fan

My mom, she listens in each day
   To ev'ry baseball game,
An' knows each player on the team
   By his own given name.

She knows each member's record an'
   His battin' av'rage, too,
An' when it comes his turn to bat,
   Just what he's gonna do.

When pitchers load the bases, Mom
   Will holler, "Take him out!"
Or tell the ump, "The rules are what
   You don't know much about."

She's pick'd up all the lingo of
   The game as it is played,
An' knows all substitutions which
   The manager has made.

My mom, she never likes to see
   A player get a walk,
An' watches all the pitchers just
   In case they make a balk.

When runners are on first an' third,
   My mom will always say
That now's the time, with one man out,
   To make a double play.

Oh, yes, indeed! My mom, she is
   An ardent baseball fan,
An' listens on the radio
   To ev'ry game she can.

Mom's Housecleanin' Time

My mom, when she's a cleanin' house
An' scrubbin' up the floors,
Says Pop an' I had better be
A stayin' out of doors.

She says, when either one of us
Starts in to helpin' her,
We never do the things that make
Her work much easier.

She'd rather do the work herself
An' know it's rightly done,
Than have to finish all the tasks
That we have each begun.

We're always gettin' in her way
With ev'rything we do,
An' make a mess for her to clean
Before the job is through.

So, that is why my mom insists,
Upon each cleanin' day,
That Pop an' I keep out of sight
An' not get in her way.

That's My Mom

My mom, she organizes all
   The jobs she has me do,
An' supervises ev'ry move
   Until each one is through.

She does a heap of thinkin' 'bout
   Each problem in advance,
An' never has been known to leave
   A single thing to chance.

If I have been assign'd to rake
   The leaves from off the yard,
She's always plann'd it when the wind
   Is never blowin' hard.

If Pop comes home at night an' wants
   To fix the garden fence,
My mom has pick'd the tools he'll need
   Before he can commence.

Indeed, it is uncanny, but
   A fact without a doubt,
That Moms are necessary things
   To always have about.

Tapestry of Love

A tapestry of love she weaves,
The pattern of her life she leaves —
First, daughter's role, then mother's place,
Then grandmother in well-earned grace —

The weave displays time stitched in rose
As joy and hope the pattern shows,
Aligned with sorrow cast in blue,
Bright orange for courage running through.

And yet, what holds the whole in place?
What is the magic thread we trace
From stitches tentative in youth
To final form of perfect truth?

What adds a texture rich and deep
To the patterns that we keep?
The answer, woven through our lives,
Must be the love in Mother's eyes.

Amanda Barrickman

Photo opposite
MAYAN INDIAN CRAFTS
H. Armstrong Roberts

Forever Young

All mothers are beautiful when they are young — remember? Then as the years turn into decades, Mother meets another man besides Dad and this man is Old Father Time. Her fresh beauty changes after she and Old Father Time get to be good friends. There are little cut lines on her thumb made by the paring knife, and the winter winds roughen her cheeks when she hangs out the clothes (even when she uses all those magic creams). She doesn't carry the grocery bags so jauntily as when you were skipping along by her side. And her eyes, once dancing, are tired because they have seen so many, many things. Then one day, Mother looks in the mirror and says to herself, "I am no longer pretty," and it is a sad and lonely day. Mother is seldom wrong, but she was wrong that time. The beauty of mothers is as indestructible as Faith, Hope, and Love because mothers are all these things and more.

When the years roll on and the children scatter to the faraway places of the earth, Mother's job is done. Her little ones have become young men and women, for better or for worse, and there is nothing left that she possibly can do. Now she can sit back and relax and take things easy in the golden autumn of her life. But does she? No! Now she has grandchildren to visit, to plan for, to buy for, to make for, to sew for, to knit for, and if she lives long enough she becomes a great-grandmother. Only then can she stop and rest and spend the remainder of her days just being as beautiful as only great-grandmothers can be.

But whether she be eighteen or eighty, Mother is an irreplaceable treasure. None other will ever love you half so well or half so foolishly. None other will be so sure you are right, good and worthy. Of course, sometimes she is wrong, but God love her for it and keep her forever in His grace.

Alan Beck

Truant Lady

No breakfast dishes have been washed;
   I haven't made a bed;
I'm strolling down my garden paths,
   Admiring blooms instead.

There's dust upon the furniture;
   I'm sure the floors aren't clean.
Enthralled, I pick another bud —
   The rarest one I've seen.

If I were prompt in household work,
   My moments would be few
In which to see the morning blooms,
   All shimmery with dew.

I've always tried to figure out
   Why umpteen household duties
Appear at hours when gardens hold
   Their most entrancing beauties!

Lyla Myers

Photo opposite
EDISTO GARDENS
South Carolina
Fred Sieb

For a Child

Your friends shall be the tall wind,
    The river and the tree;
The sun that laughs and marches,
    The swallow and the sea.

Your prayers shall be the murmur
    Of grasses in the rain;
The song of wildwood thrushes
    That makes God glad again.

And you shall run and wander
    And you shall dream and sing
Of brave things and bright things
    Beyond the swallow's wing.

And you shall envy no man,
    Nor hurt your heart with sighs,
For I will keep you simple
    That God may make you wise.

Fanny Stearns Davis

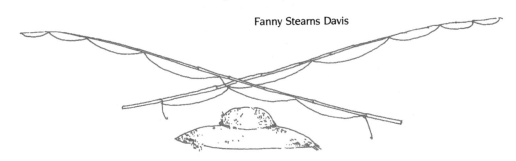

Of a Small Daughter Walking Outdoors

Easy, wind!
Go softly here!
She is small
And very dear.

She is young
And cannot say
Words to chase
The wind away.

She is new
To walking, so
Wind, be kind
And gently blow

On her ruffled head,
On grass and clover.
Easy, wind . . .
She'll tumble over!

Frances M. Frost

Photo opposite
AMERICAN PAINTED LADY
ON COLUMBINE
Gay Bumgarner

Foal

Come trotting up
Beside your mother,
Little skinny.

Lay your neck across
Her back, and whinny,
Little foal.

You think you're a horse
Because you can trot —
But you're not.

Your eyes are so wild,
And each leg is as tall
As a pole;

And you're only a skittish
Child, after all,
Little foal.

Mary Britton Miller

Flower of Spring

O flower of spring so pure and fair,
How you enchant the garden air.
I've watched you sprout from out of clay
And marveled at the mighty way
You grew more lovely every day —
    O flower of spring.

O flower of spring, though bound by sod
You turn your petaled face to God,
And in your little corner here
You spread a daily wealth of cheer
To those who may be passing near —
    O flower of spring.

O flower of spring, I've learned from you
What God would like to have me do.
You gave to me the secret of
The flowers that trust the hand above,
And grow by yielding to His love —
    O flower of spring.

O flower of spring, through you I see
The great Creator teaching me.
I, too, can grow in strength and grace,
Though anchored in a humble place,
If in my youth I seek God's face —
    O flower of spring.

Donald Laverne Walker

Photo opposite
CANADIAN DOGWOOD
Ed Cooper

Maternity

Heigh ho! daisies and buttercups,
   Fair yellow daffodils, stately and tall,
When the wind wakes, how they rock in the grasses
   And dance with the cuckoo-buds, slender and small:
Here are two bonny boys, and mother's own lasses,
   Eager to gather them all.

Heigh ho! daisies and buttercups,
    Mother shall thread them a daisy chain;
Sing them a song of the pretty hedge sparrow
    That loved her brown little ones, loved them full fain;
Sing, "Heart thou art wide though the house be but narrow" —
    Sing once, and sing it again.

Heigh ho! daisies and buttercups,
    Sweet wagging cowslips, they bend and they bow;
A ship sails afar over warm ocean waters,
    And haply one musing doth stand at her prow.
O bonny brown sons, and O sweet little daughters,
    Maybe he thinks on you now!

Heigh ho! daisies and buttercups,
    Fair yellow daffodils stately and tall;
A sunshiny world full of laughter and leisure,
    And fresh hearts unconscious of sorrow and thrall,
Send down on their pleasure smiles passing its measure —
    God that is over us all.

Jean Ingelow

The Home Planting

I have been planting all the day,
Knees to the earth and back to the sun,
Pausing, at moments, to watch the sway
Of willows where dancing breezes run,
Seeing how blue the waters shine
In the distant pond where the white ducks make
Beauty into their own design,
Following after the curl-tailed drake.

I feel the earth between spread fingers
And set out plants in a steady row —
There's a magic in this that somehow lingers
Beyond the hour, as if the glow
Of purple asters, red, and white,
And hardy sweet peas in a blaze,
And colored tulips gay with light
Could reach across the gulf of days
Between the planting and the bloom
To make the heart a lovely room!

Eleanor Halbrook Zimmerman

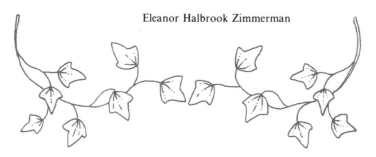

Photo opposite
HYDRANGEA
Jeff Wiles
Peregrine Photo Studio

May Day

The shining line of motors,
    The swaying motorbus,
The prancing dancing horses
    Are passing by for us.

The sunlight on the steeple,
    The toys we stop to see,
The smiling passing people
    Are all for you and me.

"I love you and I love you!" —
    "And oh, I love you, too!"
"All of the flower girl's lilies
    Were only grown for you!"

Fifth Avenue and April
    And love and lack of care —
The world is mad with music
    Too beautiful to bear.

Sara Teasdale

Reprinted with permission of Macmillan Publishing Company from RIVERS TO THE SEA by Sara Teasdale. Copyright 1915 by Macmillan Publishing Co., Inc., renewed 1943 by Mamie T. Wheless.

May Day

A delicate fabric of bird song
   Floats in the air,
The smell of wet wild earth
   Is everywhere.

Red small leaves of the maple
   Are clenched like a hand,
Like girls at their first communion
   The pear trees stand.

Oh, I must pass nothing by
   Without loving it much,
The raindrops try with my lips,
   The grass at my touch;

For how can I be sure
   I shall see again
The world on the first of May
   Shining after the rain?

Sara Teasdale

Reprinted with permission of Macmillan Publishing Company from COLLECTED POEMS by Sara Teasdale. Copyright 1920 by Macmillan Publishing Co., Inc., renewed 1948 by Mamie T. Wheless.

Overleaf
CRABAPPLE BLOSSOMS
Gene Ahrens

Herald of Spring

He is the harbinger of spring, the worm-tugger, the well-wound morning alarm clock, the builder of tight and cozy nests. He is the first bird that many people learn to recognize; his song is known across the country. Perhaps there is nothing more familiar than the American Robin.

However, in spite of his popularity, few people know the robin well. His brilliant red breast, his melodious voice, his spotted children...this is all that we may notice. Yet the robin's life is an interesting mix of many skills, and he plays each role with a unique style — from soloist to architect to parent and provider.

In the spring, robins spend their days in defending their territory, looking for a mate, in courtship, and feeding. The work varies, depending on the sex of the robin. Although the male is the one who stakes out a territory, once a partner is found, both the male and female defend their claim. That is, until nesting begins.

Then a new division of labor occurs. It is usually the female robin who chooses the nest location. The male may try to make suggestions or even hint at repairing an old nest. But the female is very fastidious about her home and rarely uses an old nest. She looks for a new site, five to twenty feet above the ground, which will provide a strong foundation. Many times

this will be a man-made structure such as a window ledge, broad fence, eaves trough, or bridge. Sometimes a firm foundation is more important than seclusion.

Once the robin has selected a suitable home site, construction begins. The male may fly in some materials to help, but the female is the principal architect. She is both particular and indecisive, however. If she likes several locations, she may begin several nests before choosing her favorite and final one.

One of the best examples of this indecision was observed in Ohio when a female robin discovered a building under construction. In the place where the roof rafters lay across a wooden girder, there were spaces for numerous nests. Which to choose? It was plainly giving her trouble. In one week's time that robin built twenty-six nests in twenty-six of those spaces. Her efforts were watched and aided by a group of amazed construction workers who provided her with mud and other nesting materials. And they couldn't resist placing bets on her final choice. She at last made it, picking one nest from all the others and raising her family there.

Most robins are more sensible, though, and select their homes with less drama. Once building begins, the project usually takes five or six days to complete. Later in the summer, other nests will be built because robins raise two or three families during a season. But these second and third nests receive less time and attention than the first.

One or two days after the nest is completed, the female begins to lay her sky-blue eggs, one each day, until there are three or four. Unless the weather has been very cold, she waits until all the eggs have been laid before beginning incubation. In that way, all eggs will hatch on the same day and no one will have the advantage of a head start. The female does the incubating, sitting on her eggs all night and most of the day. The male does not bring her food so she must take short, five or ten minute breaks to look for dinner. She is a diligent mother, giving her eggs intensive care, and turning them periodically to insure even heating and proper development.

This careful attention continues for some time. When the robin eggs finally hatch, twelve or thirteen days later, they yield a very delicate cargo. The robin nestlings are born featherless, blind, and unable to sit up. In fact, they can hold up their heads for only a few moments to grapple with food from their parents. It is hard to believe that in less than two weeks they will be fully feathered, aching for freedom, and too large to remain in the nest.

After hatching, the nestlings present their parents with an enormous demand for food. Now, at last, the father robin begins to take more interest in his family, and he quickly becomes irreplaceable. For even with both parents helping, the workload is exhausting. The growing birds eat unimaginable amounts of food: during their two weeks in the nest, their parents feed them about three pounds of material — mostly in the form of worms and insects. So great is the family's appetite that both parents must work from dawn to dusk collecting food. They make trips to the nest every five or ten minutes to refill the gaping beaks. One scientist recorded a bird who, on its last day in the nest, ate fourteen feet of earthworm!

Protecting the young robins from adverse weather is primarily the mother's job. She is indispensable when the nestlings are very young and featherless. She spends most of her time on the nest and may even interrupt her own feeding runs in order to warm her nestlings. If she is killed during this time, the father robin will have a most difficult job before him. Although he may manage to keep up with feeding the nestlings, he cannot keep them warm if bad weather threatens the nest. Nevertheless, lone robins (including fathers) have been known to successfully finish the raising of families.

When the nestlings are between ten and fourteen days old, they begin to show an interest in the world beyond the nest. They usually leave the nest one at a time, which gives the parents more opportunity to supervise things. After a young bird has toppled out or glided to the ground, both parents feed and watch out for him for a day or two. Then mother leaves to begin work on nest number two or nest number three. From here on, father robin is left in charge of the awkward youngsters, now called fledglings. For two more weeks he must follow them about, wean them, and protect them from danger. Even after the young birds are able to catch their own food, they try to beg free meals from dad. The father robin must also be alert for danger, for it is at this time that his charges are most susceptible. And dangers come from all sources, whether it be a drooling cat or a concerned human who thinks that the gawky youngster is an orphan.

The family months certainly keep the parent robins hopping, but even days filled with feeding, guarding, and teaching have their peaceful moments. As the day slowly folds up its sunlight, the young robins settle down, and there is a chance for their frenzied parents to search out a meal for themselves.

And so the robins' busy day reaches its end. Mother settles her downy feathers over her nest and young. Father ruffles his wings for his evening flight to the roost. But before he goes, there is one more touch he feels compelled to add to his day. From the top of his favorite tree he spangles the twilight with his song. Scientists will explain it as a last defensive claim of his territory before retiring for the night. But when listening to him sprinkle his silvery notes upon the evening, it is hard to feel this way. Isn't his music a serenade to his mate? After all, he first sang to call her to his home. Isn't his last song really for her? A soft reassurance of a good day past...and a promise that he'll be back soon — even before the morning sun cuts through the hills.

Mary Mercier

Mother's Love

Love is the only bow on life's dark cloud. It is the morning and evening star. It shines upon the babe, and sheds its radiance on the quiet tomb. It is the mother of art, inspirer of poet, patriot, and philosopher. It is the air and light of every heart — builder of every home, kindler of every fire on every hearth. It was the first to dream of immortality. It fills the world with melody — for music is the voice of love. Love is the magician, the enchanter, that changes worthless things to joy, and makes right royal kings and queens of common clay. It is the perfume of that wondrous flower, the heart, and without that sacred passion, that divine swoon, we are less than beasts; but with it, earth is heaven, and we are gods.

Robert G. Ingersoll

My Garden

The lilac in my garden comes to bloom;
   The apple, plum and cherry wait their hour,
The honeysuckle climbs from pole to pole —
   And the rockery has a stone that's now a flower,
Jeweled by moss in every tiny hole!

Close to my lilac there's a small bird's nest
   Of quiet, young, half-sleeping birds: but when
I look, each little rascal — five I've reckoned —
   Opens a mouth so large and greedy then,
He swallows his own face in half a second!

W. H. Davies

Mother's Lilacs

Dear trysting winds, bring me the
    fragrance tonight
Of sweet-scented lilacs in purple
    and blue.
Take me again to an old-fashioned
    garden
Where lilacs are dripping with
    silvery dew.
There let me linger awhile in the
    moonlight
To dream of my mother and see
    her dear face,
Framed mid the beauty of sweet-
    scented lilacs,
For this was her garden
    time will not erase.

Caroline Henning Bair

Blossom-Time

There's a wedding in the orchard, dear,
   I know it by the flowers:
They're wreathed on every bough and branch,
   Or falling down in showers.

The air is in a mist, I think,
   And scarce knows which to be —
Whether all fragrance, clinging close,
   Or birdsong, wild and free.

And countless wedding jewels shine,
   And golden gifts of grace:
I never saw such wealth of sun
   In any shady place.

It seemed I heard the flutt'ring robes
   Of maidens clad in white,
The clasping of a thousand hands
   In tenderest delight;

While whispers ran among the boughs
   Of promises and praise;
And playful, loving messages
   Sped through the leaf-lit ways.

And just beyond the wreathed aisles
   That end against the blue,
The raiment of the wedding choir
   And priest came shining through.

And though I saw no wedding guest,
   Nor groom, nor gentle bride,
I know that holy things were asked,
   And holy love replied.

And something through the sunlight said:
   "Let all who love be blest!
The earth is wedded to the spring —
   And God, He knoweth best."

Mary E. Dodge

Photo opposite
BUDDHA'S TEMPLE
Avery Island
Ed Cooper

Green Things Growing

Oh, the green things growing,
The green things growing,
The faint, sweet smell
Of the green things growing!
I should like to live,
Whether I smile or grieve,
Just to watch the happy life
Of my green things growing.

Oh, the fluttering and the pattering
Of those green things growing!
How they talk each to each,
When none of us are knowing;
In the wonderful white
Of the weird moonlight
Or the dim dreamy dawn
When the cocks are crowing.

I love, I love them so, —
My green things growing!
And I think that they love me,
Without false showing;
For by many a tender touch,
They comfort me so much,
With the soft, mute comfort
Of green things growing.

Dinah Maria Mulock

June
Is Coming

I knew that you were coming, June,
   I knew that you were coming!
Among the alders by the stream
   I heard a partridge drumming;
I heard a partridge drumming, June,
   a welcome with his wings,
And felt softness in the air —
   half summer's and half spring's.

I knew that you were nearing, June,
   I knew that you were nearing —
I saw it in the bursting buds
   of roses in the clearing;
The roses in the clearing, June,
   were blushing pink and red,
For they had heard upon the hills
   the echo of your tread.

I knew that you were coming, June,
   I knew that you were coming,
For ev'ry warbler in the wood
   a song of joy was humming.
I know that you are here, June,
   I know that you are here —
The fairy month, the merry month,
   the laughter of the year!

Douglas Malloch

Ideals Pays Tribute to Friends Old and New!

Ideals pays tribute to cherished companions and dearest friends in our next issue, FRIENDSHIP IDEALS.

Through our stunning color photography and heartwarming poetry and prose, we invite you to enjoy a picnic at the beach with a special friend, savor a moment of solitude with nature, chuckle at the antics of animal friends, cherish good books like old friends.

But let our friends, loyal Ideals readers, tell you more: "Your magazine symbolizes all that I hold dear in the world: love of God, country, family, and friends. God bless you all" (N. M., Warner Robins, Georgia). "I received a subscription to your publication as a gift and I love it! Its warmth and beauty are truly a collector's piece which I keep and show off next to my collection of rare and unique books.... As a poet, I enjoy the quality and diversity you provide — and my family and guests enjoy it every bit as much as I do" (L. A., Bakersfield, California).

We invite you to extend the hand of friendship to a special person in your life today — with a gift subscription, beginning with FRIENDSHIP IDEALS.

ACKNOWLEDGMENTS

MOTHER'S LILACS by Caroline Henning Bair, reprinted by permission of Patricia J. Bair; HER HEART'S AT HOME from THE HEART OF HOME by Anne Campbell, copyright 1931 by The John C. Winston Co., Philadelphia; the poem WYNKEN, BLYNKEN, AND NOD by Eugene Field and accompanying artwork from ONCE UPON A RHYME, copyright © 1978 by Ideals Publishing Corporation; WHAT MOTHER IS from IN PRAISE OF MOTHERS by J. Harold Gwynne; FLOWERS FOR MOTHER'S DAY by Elizabeth Searle Lamb first published in CAPPER'S WEEKLY; JUNE IS COMING by Douglas Malloch from THE YEAR AROUND: POEMS FOR CHILDREN, copyright 1956 by Abingdon Press, courtesy of Robert Hill; MOM'S HOUSECLEANIN' TIME, MY MOM'S A BASEBALL FAN, and THAT'S MY MOM from FIVE TIMES TWENTY, copyright 1949 by Fred Toothaker; NEEDS by Charles Hanson Towne from THE DESK DRAWER ANTHOLOGY, copyright 1937 by Doubleday, Doran & Company, Inc.; MOTHER-PRAYER by Margaret Widdemer from her book THE OLD ROAD TO PARADISE AND OTHER POEMS, copyright 1946, reprinted by permission of John D. Widdemer. Our sincere thanks to the following people whose addresses we were unable to locate: Fanny Stearns Davis for FOR A CHILD from MY POETRY BOOK, copyright © 1962, Holt, Rinehart and Winston Publishers; Ona Jane Meens for IRIS from her book FRAGMENTS OF LIFE, copyright 1965; Lyla Myers for TRUANT LADY; Saxon White Uberuaga for LIFE'S A PUZZLE; and Eleanor Halbrook Zimmerman for THE HOME PLANTING.